VEGETARIAN
Pasta
RECIPES

A QUANTUM BOOK

Published by
Selectabook Limited
Devizes

ISBN 1-86160-031-3

This book was produced by
Quantum Books Ltd
6 Blundell Street
London N7 9BH

Produced in Australia by Griffin Colour

VEGETARIAN Pasta RECIPES

Pasta Dough

This is the basic recipe referred to throughout the book. The dough can be made up to 2 days in advance, if kept airtight in the fridge. Bring the dough to room temperature before rolling out.

Freezing pasta is best done after it has been rolled out and cut into the required shape. Cook from frozen, allowing a little extra cooking time for stuffed pasta shapes.

MAKES ABOUT 550G/1¼LB

350g/12oz strong plain flour

1tbsp salt

60ml/4tbsp sunflower oil

12ml/1tbsp water

3 eggs

1

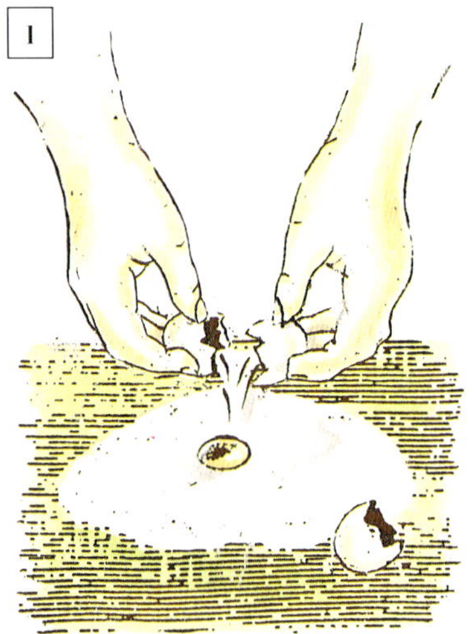

In a large mixing bowl, combine the flour and salt. Make a well in the centre. In a mixing jug, combine the sunflower oil and water and beat well. Break the eggs into the well and add the oil and water mixture gradually. Mix until the dough forms clumps.

2

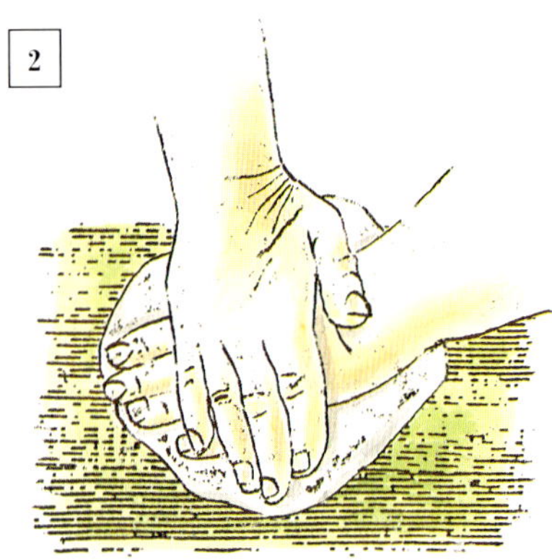

Turn out on to a lightly floured surface and knead the dough for about 5 minutes, adding the minimum amount of extra flour to stop the dough sticking, if necessary.

Place the dough in a polythene bag or seal in clingfilm and leave to rest, at room temperature, for at least 30 minutes.

3

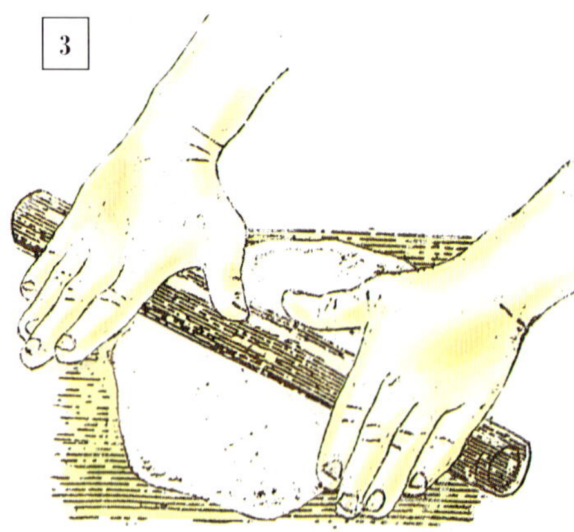

Roll out the dough and cut to any shape you require.

TIPS FOR COOKING PERFECT PASTA:

- Use good-quality pasta.
- Use a saucepan which is large enough to hold the pasta with the water and still have at least one third of the saucepan free.
- Bring the water to the boil before adding the pasta, then simmer for the duration of the cooking time.
- Add a dash of oil to the cooking water to help prevent the pasta sticking together.
- Cook the pasta until *al dente*, or tender.
- To halt the cooking process, drain the pasta through a sieve and rinse under cold running water.

BASIC SAUCES

These basic sauces are used in recipes throughout the book. However, they can also be used as recipes in their own right, poured over or mixed into your favourite pasta shapes. Made up to two days in advance and kept, covered in the refrigerator, the sauces can be reheated for use in the recipes.

Cheese Sauce

This sauce will keep in the fridge covered, for up to a week. Use for lasagnes, bakes, toppings and fillings.

MAKES ABOUT 575ML/1PT

- 25g/1oz butter or margarine
- 25g/1oz plain flour
- 575ml/1pt warm milk
- 5ml/1tsp Dijon mustard
- 100g/4oz grated mature Cheddar cheese
- salt and freshly ground black pepper

Melt the butter or margarine in a medium-sized saucepan and stir in the flour. Cook for 30 seconds then remove from the heat.

Stir in the milk, a little at a time, blending well after each addition to prevent any lumps. Return the sauce to a medium heat and stir constantly until the sauce thickens and boils.

Add the mustard and cheese and season to taste with salt and freshly ground black pepper. Continue to cook, stirring constantly, until the cheese has melted.

VARIATIONS:

MUSHROOM SAUCE Omit the mustard and cheese and stir in 175g/6oz chopped button mushrooms which have been sautéed in a little olive oil with a clove of crushed garlic and a pinch of dried thyme.

TOMATO SAUCE Omit the mustard and cheese and stir in 45ml/3tbsp tomato purée.

Pesto Sauce

This traditional Italian sauce should be used in moderation as it has a very strong flavour. Delicious stirred into fresh pasta, Pesto Sauce can also be used as an ingredient, added to other sauces and dishes. The texture of the finished pesto can be left quite coarse or puréed until smooth.

SERVES 4–6

2 cloves of garlic, crushed

8tbsp chopped fresh basil

2tbsp chopped fresh parsley

50g/2oz pine nuts

75g/3oz fresh grated Parmesan cheese

150ml/¼pt extra virgin olive oil

salt and freshly ground black pepper

Place all the ingredients in a food processor or blender and blend until the pesto reaches the desired texture.

Stir Pesto Sauce into freshly cooked pasta tossed in butter and freshly ground black pepper. Serve immediately with extra freshly grated Parmesan cheese.

TIP:

For a more traditional method of preparation, place all the ingredients in a mortar and use the pestle to grind and pound until the pesto reaches the desired texture.

Cream Sauce

An excellent standby sauce for any occasion. It is delicious served with spaghetti or used as a foundation for other ingredients to make a more elaborate dish.

SERVES 4

2 cloves of garlic, crushed

3tbsp chopped fresh parsley

275ml/½pt single cream

salt and freshly ground black pepper

Place all the ingredients in a medium-sized frying pan and cook over low heat for 5–8 minutes, stirring occasionally.

SERVING SUGGESTION:

Stir Cream Sauce into freshly cooked tagliatelle verde and serve immediately with plenty of freshly grated Parmesan cheese.

Herby Mushroom Pasta Salad

Any small pasta shapes would be suitable for this dish. It can be served as a filling main course at lunchtime or as an accompaniment.

SERVES 4–8

- 450g/1lb dried pasta shapes
- dash of olive oil
- 225g/8oz cup mushrooms, quartered
- 1 red pepper, seeded and cut into 1cm/½inch squares
- 1 yellow pepper, seeded and cut into 1cm/½inch squares
- 100g/4oz pitted black olives
- 4tbsp chopped fresh basil
- 2tbsp chopped fresh parsley

FOR THE DRESSING:

- 10ml/2tsp red wine vinegar
- 1tsp salt
- freshly ground black pepper
- 60ml/4tbsp extra virgin olive oil
- 1 clove of garlic, crushed
- 5–10ml/1–2tsp Dijon mustard

Bring a large saucepan of water to the boil and add the pasta shapes with a dash of olive oil. Cook for about 10 minutes, stirring occasionally, until tender. Drain and rinse under cold running water. Drain well again.

Place the cooked pasta shapes in a large salad bowl and add the remaining salad ingredients. Mix well to combine.

To make the dressing, place all the ingredients in a screw-top jar and shake well. Pour the dressing over the salad and toss together.

Cover and refrigerate for at least 30 minutes, then toss again before serving.

Pasta-topped Mushrooms

This dish is delicious served cold with a crisp leafy salad or warm as a starter or an accompaniment. The topping can be made in advance and arranged on the mushrooms at the last minute.

SERVES 2–4

50g/2oz dried small stellette (stars)

dash of olive oil

4 large flat mushrooms

50g/2oz butter

1 clove of garlic, crushed

½ yellow pepper, seeded and finely diced

½ orange pepper, seeded and finely diced

150g/5oz blue cheese, such as Stilton or Danish blue, crumbled

salt and freshly ground black pepper

2tbsp chopped fresh parsley

Bring a large saucepan of water to the boil and add the stellette with a dash of olive oil. Cook for about 7 minutes, stirring occasionally, until tender. Drain and set aside.

Cut the stalks out of the mushrooms and discard. Arrange the mushrooms, stalk side up, on a baking sheet and set aside.

To make the topping, melt the butter in a frying pan and sauté the garlic for about 2 minutes. Add the diced peppers and cook for a further 5–7 minutes. Stir in the crumbled blue cheese and season to taste with salt and freshly ground black pepper. Add the parsley and stellette. Stir well.

Top each mushroom with the pasta mixture then place the baking sheet under a hot grill for 2–5 minutes, or until the topping is lightly golden and the mushrooms are warmed through.

Tagliatelle with Mushrooms

A quick supper for any occasion. Try using spaghetti or linguini for a change.

SERVES 4

450g/1lb dried tagliatelle

dash of olive oil

25g/1oz butter

1 clove of garlic, crushed

2tbsp chopped fresh parsley

225g/8oz button or cup mushrooms, sliced

salt and freshly ground black pepper

275ml/½pt single cream

freshly grated Parmesan cheese, to serve

Bring a large saucepan of water to the boil and add the tagliatelle with a dash of olive oil. Cook for about 10 minutes, stirring occasionally, until tender. Drain and set aside.

Meanwhile, melt the butter in a large frying pan and sauté the garlic and chopped parsley for 2–3 minutes. Add the sliced mushrooms and cook for 5–8 minutes, or until softened and slightly browned.

Season the mushroom mixture with salt and freshly ground black pepper, then stir in the cream. Cook the sauce for 1–2 minutes, then stir in the tagliatelle. Continue to cook while stirring to coat the tagliatelle in the sauce. Serve with plenty of freshly grated Parmesan cheese.

OPPOSITE *Pasta-topped Mushrooms*

Fusilli with Wild Mushrooms

Wild mushrooms, or ceps, are increasingly available and are the special ingredient in this dish. Dried ceps can be found in Italian delicatessens; they need to be soaked in water for 30 minutes before using in the recipe.

SERVES 4

- 325g/11oz dried long fusilli (twists)
- dash of olive oil plus 75ml/5tbsp
- 1 clove of garlic, crushed
- 2tbsp chopped fresh thyme
- 150g/5oz fresh shiitake mushrooms, sliced
- 150g/5oz fresh oyster mushrooms
- 15g/½oz dried ceps, soaked, drained and sliced
- salt and freshly ground black pepper
- freshly grated Parmesan cheese, to serve

Bring a large saucepan of water to the boil and add the fusilli with a dash of olive oil. Cook for about 10 minutes, stirring occasionally, until tender. Drain and set aside, covered.

Heat the olive oil in a large frying pan and add the garlic and fresh thyme. Cook for 1–2 minutes, then stir in all the mushrooms and season to taste with salt and freshly ground black pepper.

Fry the mushroom mixture over high heat for 3–4 minutes to brown slightly, then turn the mixture into the saucepan containing the fusilli. Toss together briefly, then serve with a little freshly grated Parmesan cheese.

Cheesy Mushroom Canapés

These tasty morsels are ideal for entertaining. They can be made in advance and are delicious served with drinks.

SERVES 8–10

20 dried large lumache rigate or large shells

dash of olive oil

3tbsp freshly grated Parmesan cheese

FOR THE FILLING:

30ml/2tbsp olive oil

1 clove of garlic, chopped

1 small onion, finely chopped

3tbsp chopped fresh parsley

175g/6oz button mushrooms, very finely chopped

50g/2oz pitted olives, very finely chopped

225g/8oz full-fat soft cheese

salt and freshly ground black pepper

Bring a large saucepan of water to the boil and add the pasta with a dash of olive oil. Cook for about 10 minutes, stirring occasionally, until tender. Drain and rinse under cold running water. Pat dry with absorbent kitchen paper and set aside.

To make the filling, heat the oil in a large frying pan and sauté the garlic and onion for about 3 minutes, until softened. Remove from the heat and stir in the remaining filling ingredients.

Use a teaspoon to stuff each pasta shape with the filling and arrange them on a baking sheet. Sprinkle with grated Parmesan cheese and place under a hot grill for about 5 minutes until golden. Arrange on a serving plate.

Pinwheel Pasta Bake.

Pinwheel Pasta Bake

A homely dish that is perfect for a family supper. This is a good recipe for the freezer. When thawed, reheat, covered, in a medium-hot oven.

SERVES 4–6

675g/1½lb dried rotelle (pinwheels)

dash of olive oil

30ml/2tbsp sunflower oil

1 clove of garlic, crushed

225g/8oz mushrooms, quartered

100g/4oz courgettes, chopped

3tbsp chopped fresh parsley

150ml/¼pt vegetable stock

175g/6oz grated mature Cheddar cheese

Bring a large saucepan of water to the boil and add the rotelle with a dash of olive oil. Cook for about 10 minutes, sitrring occasionally, until tender. Drain and set aside.

Heat the sunflower oil in a large frying pan and sauté the garlic for 2 minutes. Add the mushrooms and courgettes and cook, covered, for 5 minutes, or until softened.

Stir the chopped parsley and vegetable stock into the mushroom mixture and continue to cook, covered, for a further 10 minutes. Add the rotelle and stir in the grated cheese.

Preheat the oven to 200°C/400°F/Gas Mark 6. Transfer the pasta mixture to a deep casserole dish and bake for about 20 minutes. Serve with warm crusty bread.

Hearty Cream of Mushroom Soup

Perfect for a cold winter's night or even a filling lunchtime dish. Serve with warm, crusty garlic bread for a more substantial meal.

SERVES 4

25g/1oz butter

1 onion, finely chopped

350g/12oz cup mushrooms, finely chopped

1tbsp plain flour

575ml/1pt vegetable stock

275ml/½pt milk

salt and freshly ground black pepper

100g/4oz cooked tiny pasta shapes

pinch of freshly grated nutmeg

Melt the butter in a large saucepan and sauté the onion for about 3 minutes until softened. Add the chopped mushrooms, cover and cook for a further 5 minutes.

Stir in the flour, then gradually add the stock and milk, stirring well after each addition. Cover and cook for 15–20 minutes, stirring occasionally. Season with salt and freshly ground black pepper. Stir in the pasta shapes and grated nutmeg. Cook for a final 2–3 minutes, then serve.

Bucatini with Tomatoes

This is a vegetarian version of a simple yet classic Italian dish. Use Parmesan cheese if Pecorino is not available.

SERVES 4

- 350g/12oz dried bucatini (long tubes)
- dash of olive oil
- 2 cloves of garlic, crushed
- 1 onion, finely chopped
- 450g/1lb carton sieved tomatoes
- 4tbsp chopped fresh basil
- salt and freshly ground black pepper
- butter, for greasing
- 50g/2oz freshly grated Pecorino or Parmesan cheese

Bring a large saucepan of water to the boil and add the bucatini with a dash of olive oil. Cook for about 10 minutes, stirring occasionally, until tender. Drain and set aside.

Preheat the oven to 200°C/400°F/Gas Mark 6. Place the garlic, onion, sieved tomatoes, basil and salt and freshly ground black pepper in a large frying pan and heat until simmering. Cook for about 5 minutes, then remove from the heat.

Arrange the bucatini in a shallow, buttered ovenproof dish. Curl it round to fit the dish, adding one or two tubes at a time, until the dish is tightly packed with the pasta.

Spoon over the tomato mixture, prodding and poking the pasta to ensure the sauce sinks down to the bottom of the dish. Sprinkle the grated cheese over the top and bake for 25–30 minutes, until bubbling, crisp and golden. Cut in wedges, like a cake, to serve.

Tagliatelle Neapolitan

Yellow tomatoes make this dish look particularly attractive, though red ones taste just as good. If you can't find fresh tagliatelle, use the dried egg version.

SERVES 4

- 450g/1lb fresh multi-coloured tagliatelle
- dash of olive oil, plus 30ml/2tbsp
- 2 cloves of garlic, crushed
- 1 onion, chopped
- 3tbsp chopped fresh basil or oregano
- 450g/1lb yellow and red tomatoes, skinned, seeded and chopped
- 225g/8oz carton sieved tomatoes
- salt and freshly ground black pepper
- fresh basil, to garnish
- freshly grated Parmesan cheese, to serve

Bring a large saucepan of water to the boil and add the tagliatelle with a dash of olive oil. Cook for about 5 minutes, stirring occasionally, until tender. Drain and set aside, covered.

Heat the remaining oil in a large frying pan and sauté the garlic, onion and basil or oregano for about 3 minutes, or until the onion has softened.

Add the chopped tomato flesh and sieved tomatoes and season with salt and freshly ground black pepper. Stir and cook for about 10 minutes, until thickened and bubbling. Serve with the tagliatelle. Garnish with fresh basil and sprinkle with freshly grated Parmesan cheese.

Fusilli with Sun-dried Tomatoes

A dish that is delicious served warm as a main course or cold as a summer salad. Tomato pesto is widely available.

SERVES 2–4

- 450g/1lb dried fusilli (twists)
- dash of olive oil, plus extra for drizzling
- 30ml/2tbsp tomato pesto
- 175g/6oz sun-dried tomatoes, drained and chopped
- 4 plum tomatoes, sliced into wedges
- 4tbsp chopped fresh basil
- salt and freshly ground black pepper

Bring a large saucepan of water to the boil and add the fusilli with a dash of olive oil. Cook for about 10 minutes, stirring occasionally, until tender. Drain and return to the saucepan.

Stir in the remaining ingredients, drizzle with olive oil and serve warm immediately, or cool and refrigerate to serve chilled if preferred.

OPPOSITE *Fusilli with Sun-dried Tomatoes.*

Spicy Stuffed Tomatoes

Beefsteak tomatoes are perfect for stuffing. Serve as a vegetable accompaniment or as a starter. To make the tomatoes stand up in the dish, slice a thin shaving off the bottom of each one.

SERVES 4

- 100g/4oz dried pastina (any tiny shapes)
- dash of olive oil
- 4 large beefsteak tomatoes
- butter, for greasing

FOR THE FILLING:

- 350g/12oz potatoes, cut into 5mm/¼inch cubes
- 60ml/4tbsp olive oil
- 2 cloves of garlic, crushed
- 1 onion, finely chopped
- 2tsp mild curry powder
- pinch of ground cumin
- 15ml/1tbsp tomato purée
- 4tbsp chopped fresh coriander
- salt and freshly ground black pepper

Bring a saucepan of water to the boil and add the pastina with a dash of olive oil. Cook for about 8 minutes, stirring occasionally, until tender. Drain and set aside.

Slice the tops off the tomatoes and reserve for the lids. Using a teaspoon, scrape out the flesh of each tomato and reserve. Arrange the hollowed tomatoes in a buttered ovenproof dish and set aside.

To make the filling, cook the potatoes in boiling water for about 10 minutes, until tender. Drain and set aside. Heat the olive oil in a large frying pan and sauté the garlic and onion for about 3 minutes, until softened.

Add the curry powder, cumin and tomato purée. Cook for 2 minutes, then gently stir in the pastina and cooked potato. Add the chopped coriander and season with salt and freshly ground black pepper. Cook for a further 2–3 minutes, stirring occasionally, then remove from the heat.

Preheat the oven to 200°C/400°F/Gas Mark 6. Stuff the tomatoes with the filling, placing any extra in the bottom of the dish. Place the tomato lids on top and bake for about 20 minutes, or until heated through.

Italian Spaghettini

Italian Spaghettini

Pine nuts give this dish its special taste and texture. Serve it straight from the pan.

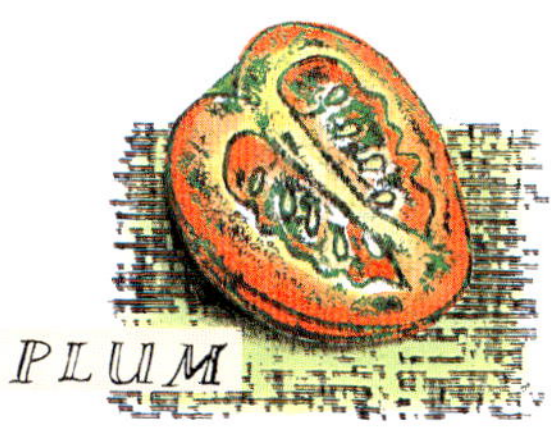

SERVES 4

- 450g/1lb dried multi-coloured spaghettini
- dash of olive oil
- 50g/2oz butter
- 1 clove of garlic, crushed
- 1 small onion, very finely chopped
- 75g/3oz pine nuts
- 225g/8oz carton sieved tomatoes
- salt and freshly ground black pepper
- 4tbsp chopped fresh basil
- 2tbsp chopped fresh parsley

Bring a large saucepan of water to the boil and add the dried spaghettini with a dash of olive oil. Cook for about 10 minutes, stirring occasionally, until tender. Drain and set aside.

Melt the butter in a large frying pan and sauté the garlic and onion for about 3 minutes, or until the onion has softened. Add the pine nuts and stir-fry until evenly golden.

Add the sieved tomatoes, salt and freshly ground black pepper and herbs and cook for about 5 minutes, stirring occasionally.

Add the spaghettini and stir well to coat in the tomato sauce. Cook for a further 5 minutes, then serve immediately.

Fettuccine with Tomatoes and Mozzarella

This delicious summertime salad can be made well in advance and left to marinate for up to 3 hours.

SERVES 4

- 350g/12oz dried egg fettuccine
- dash of olive oil
- 450g/1lb beefsteak tomatoes, skinned, seeded and sliced
- 75ml/5tbsp extra virgin olive oil
- 2 cloves of garlic, crushed
- 6tbsp chopped fresh basil
- 2tbsp chopped fresh oregano
- 350g/12oz mozzarella cheese, cut into 1cm/½inch cubes
- 50g/2oz freshly grated Pecorino or Parmesan cheese
- salt and freshly ground black pepper

Bring a large saucepan of water to the boil and add the fettuccine with a dash of olive oil. Cook for about 10 minutes, stirring occasionally, until tender. Drain and rinse under cold running water. Drain again and set aside.

In a large bowl, combine the sliced tomato flesh with the remaining ingredients and toss together lightly. Add the cooked fettuccine and mix lightly to coat in the oil. Serve this salad at room temperature with warm garlic bread.

Tomato Mozzarella Kebabs

These are excellent for a vegetarian barbecue. Serve the kebabs with plenty of hot, crusty garlic bread and salad.

SERVES 4

- 100g/4oz dried rotelle (pinwheels)
- dash of olive oil, plus 60ml/4tbsp
- 2 cloves of garlic, crushed
- salt and freshly ground black pepper
- 8–12 cherry tomatoes
- 225g/8oz mozzarella cheese, cut into 2.5cm/1inch cubes

Bring a large saucepan of water to the boil and add the rotelle with a dash of olive oil. Cook for about 10 minutes, stirring occasionally, until tender. Drain and rinse under cold running water. Drain again and set aside.

In a small bowl, combine the olive oil, garlic and salt and freshly ground black pepper. Set aside.

To make the kebabs, place one rotelle, a tomato, then a cube of mozzarella cheese on to kebab skewers until all the ingredients have been used. Arrange the skewers on a baking sheet and brush liberally with the garlic olive oil mixture, turning the kebabs to coat evenly.

Place the kebabs under a preheated grill for 5–7 minutes, turning the skewers halfway through cooking, until browned. Serve immediately.

TIP:

If using wooden skewers, soak them for at least one hour in water before threading on the kebab ingredients. This will help prevent them from burning during grilling.

Spaghettini with Tomato Ragout

This version of ragout is a brilliant standby sauce to use when hunger won't wait for time.

SERVES 4

- 450g/1lb dried spaghettini
- dash of olive oil
- freshly grated Parmesan cheese, to serve

FOR THE RAGOUT:

- 25g/1oz butter
- 1 clove of garlic, crushed
- 1 large onion, finely chopped
- 400g/14oz can chopped tomatoes
- 150ml/¼pt dry red wine
- 4tbsp chopped fresh basil
- salt and freshly ground black pepper

Bring a large saucepan of water to the boil and add the spaghettini with a dash of olive oil. Cook for about 10 minutes, stirring occasionally, until tender. Drain and set aside, covered, to keep warm.

To make the ragout, melt the butter in a large frying pan and sauté the garlic and onion for about 3 minutes, until softened. Add the remaining ragout ingredients, stir and simmer for 15 minutes, until slightly thickened. Serve with the spaghettini, sprinkled with freshly grated Parmesan cheese.

OPPOSITE *Tomato Mozzarella Kebabs.*

Stuffed Peppers

A refreshing alternative to rice, pasta makes a perfect filling for peppers. Tiny pasta shapes also work well in this dish. Serve with a crisp green salad.

SERVES 4

225g/8oz gnocchetti sardi (small dumpling shapes)

dash of olive oil

4 peppers, for stuffing

flat leaf parsley sprigs, to garnish

FOR THE FILLING:

50g/2oz butter

6 spring onions, finely chopped

2 cloves of garlic, crushed

1 pepper, seeded and finely diced

salt and freshly ground black pepper

50g/2oz freshly grated Parmesan cheese

Bring a large saucepan of water to the boil and add the gnocchetti sardi with a dash of olive oil. Cook for about 10 minutes, stirring occasionally, until tender. Drain and set aside.

Preheat the oven to 200°C/400°F/Gas Mark 6. Lay each pepper on its side and slice off the top, reserving it to make the lid. Scoop out the seeds and pith and discard. Arrange the hollowed-out peppers in a shallow ovenproof dish and set aside.

To make the filling, melt the butter in a large frying pan and sauté the spring onions and garlic for about 2 minutes, then add the diced pepper. Season with salt and freshly ground black pepper and cook for about 5 minutes, stirring occasionally.

Add the gnocchetti and the Parmesan cheese to the filling mixture and cook for about 2 minutes to heat through. Using a dessertspoon, stuff each pepper with the pasta filling, scattering any extra around the edges.

Place the pepper lids in the dish and bake for about 30 minutes, until the peppers have softened. Place under a hot grill for 2–3 minutes, if wished, just before serving, to char the pepper skins. Serve garnished with parsley sprigs.

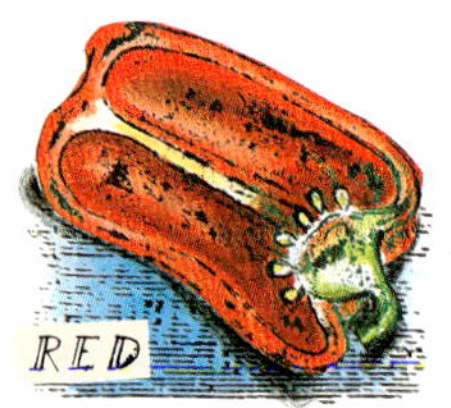

Pepper and Pasta Ratatouille.

Pepper and Pasta Ratatouille

Delicious served with a hot, buttered baked potato, this dish makes perfect bonfire-night fare.

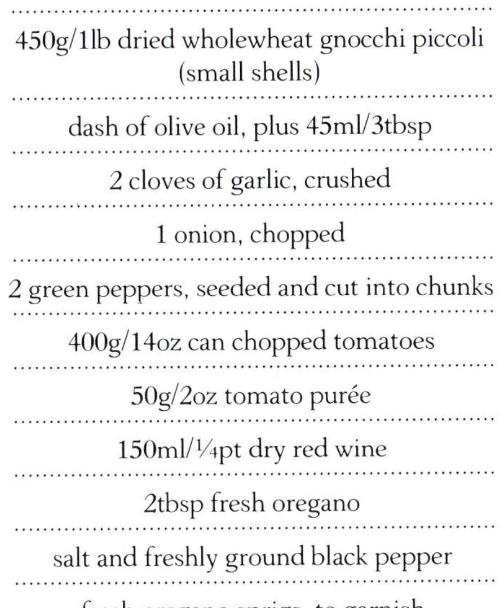

SERVES 4–6

- 450g/1lb dried wholewheat gnocchi piccoli (small shells)
- dash of olive oil, plus 45ml/3tbsp
- 2 cloves of garlic, crushed
- 1 onion, chopped
- 2 green peppers, seeded and cut into chunks
- 400g/14oz can chopped tomatoes
- 50g/2oz tomato purée
- 150ml/¼pt dry red wine
- 2tbsp fresh oregano
- salt and freshly ground black pepper
- fresh oregano sprigs, to garnish

Bring a large saucepan of water to the boil and add the gnocchi piccoli with a dash of olive oil. Cook for about 10 minutes, stirring occasionally, until tender. Drain and set aside.

Heat the remaining olive oil in a large saucepan and sauté the garlic and onion for about 3 minutes, until softened. Stir in the pepper chunks. Cover and cook for about 5 minutes, or until the pepper has softened slightly.

Stir in the remaining ingredients, except the oregano sprigs, into the pepper mixture and bring to simmering point. Reduce the heat, cover and cook for about 10 minutes, then stir in the gnocchi piccoli. Cook for a further 5 minutes, stirring occasionally. Serve garnished with fresh oregano sprigs.

Pasta with Pepper Sauce and Olives

This low-fat Pepper Sauce helps to keep the calories in this dish down. As long as the pasta used is dairy-free, this dish is also suitable for vegans.

SERVES 4

- 375g/13oz dried rigatoni (short tubes)
- dash of olive oil
- 50g/2oz stoned black olives, roughly chopped
- grated Cheddar cheese, to serve

FOR THE PEPPER SAUCE:

- 2 red peppers, skinned, seeded and roughly chopped
- 4 cloves of garlic, peeled
- 275g/½pt vegetable stock
- salt and freshly ground black pepper

Bring a large saucepan of water to the boil and add the rigatoni with a dash of olive oil. Cook for about 10 minutes, stirring occasionally, until tender. Drain and return to the saucepan. Set aside.

To make the sauce, place the chopped pepper, garlic and vegetable stock in a food processor or blender and season with salt and freshly ground black pepper. Purée until smooth.

Stir the Pepper Sauce into the rigatoni with the chopped olives. Serve with grated Cheddar cheese.

Tortellini, Peppers and Pine Nut Salad

Red peppers can be used instead of chilli peppers, if you prefer. For best results allow the salad to chill for at least an hour before serving.

SERVES 4–6

275g/10oz fresh tortellini

dash of olive oil

1 onion, very finely sliced

1 green pepper, seeded and very finely diced

75g/3oz toasted pine nuts

1 red chilli pepper, seeded and sliced (optional)

10cm/4inch piece of cucumber, very thinly sliced

1 orange, peeled and very thinly sliced

FOR THE DRESSING:

60ml/4tbsp olive oil

30ml/2tbsp sweet soya sauce

30ml/2tbsp vinegar

salt and freshly ground black pepper

Bring a large saucepan of water to the boil and add the tortellini with a dash of olive oil. Cook for about 4 minutes, stirring occasionally, until tender. Drain and rinse under cold running water. Drain again and set aside.

Place the tortellini in a large mixing bowl and add the remaining salad ingredients. Toss together lightly.

To make the salad dressing, place the ingredients in a screw-top jar and shake well to combine. Pour the dressing over the salad, toss and serve.

Rigatoni with Peppers and Garlic

The raw garlic added at the end of the recipe gives this dish the true taste of the Mediterranean.

SERVES 4

350g/12oz dried rigatoni (large tubes)

dash of olive oil, plus 60ml/4tbsp

1 large onion, chopped

4 cloves of garlic, finely chopped

2 large red peppers, seeded and roughly chopped

2 large yellow peppers, seeded and roughly chopped

2tsp chopped fresh thyme

salt and freshly ground black pepper

Bring a large saucepan of water to the boil and add the rigatoni with a dash of olive oil. Cook for about 10 minutes, stirring occasionally, until tender. Drain and set aside.

Heat the remaining oil in a large frying pan. Add the onion, 2 cloves of garlic, peppers and thyme. Cook over a medium heat for 10–15 minutes, stirring occasionally, until the vegetables are tender and beginning to brown.

Add the pasta shapes to the pepper mixture. Stir in the remaining garlic and seasoning. Serve immediately.

Tortellini, Peppers and Pine Nut Salad.

Pimiento Pasta

A quick store-cupboard recipe for a last-minute supper surprise.

SERVES 4

350g/12oz dried spaghettini

dash of olive oil, plus 30ml/2tbsp

2 cloves of garlic, crushed

400g/14oz can red pimiento, thinly sliced

salt and freshly ground black pepper

freshly grated Parmesan cheese, to serve (optional)

Bring a large saucepan of water to the boil and add the spaghettini with a dash of olive oil. Cook for about 10 minutes, stirring occasionally, until tender. Drain and return to the saucepan. Set aside, covered, to keep warm.

Heat the remaining olive oil in a frying pan and add the garlic and sliced pimiento. Stir-fry for 3–5 minutes, then tip into the warm spaghettini. Stir to combine. Serve with a little freshly grated Parmesan cheese, if wished.

Pasta with Green Peppers and Pesto

If linguini is unavailable, spaghettini or tagliatelle will work just as well in this dish.

SERVES 4

450g/1lb fresh linguini (thin, flat strips)

dash of olive oil, plus 30ml/2tbsp

2 cloves of garlic, crushed

½ quantity Pesto Sauce (page 10)

50ml/2floz vegetable stock

1 green pepper, seeded and very thinly sliced

fresh herbs, to garnish

Bring a large saucepan of water to the boil and add the linguini with a dash of olive oil. Cook for about 4 minutes, stirring occasionally, until tender. Drain and return to the saucepan. Stir in a dash more olive oil and set aside, covered, to keep warm.

Heat the remaining olive oil in a large frying pan and sauté the garlic for 1–2 minutes, then stir in the Pesto Sauce. Add the vegetable stock, stir and cook for 1 minute, then add the pepper slices. Cook for a further 7–10 minutes, stirring occasionally, until the pepper has softened. Stir the pepper mixture into the linguini and serve, garnished with fresh herbs.

Fusilli with Roasted Peppers.

Fusilli with Roasted Peppers

To prevent the pasta from sticking together, wash off the starchy cooking liquid by rinsing the pasta under boiling water from the kettle. Continue as directed in the recipe.

SERVES 4–6

- 450g/1lb dried long fusilli
- dash of olive oil
- 2 yellow peppers, seeded and cut into chunks
- 3 cloves of garlic, crushed
- 50ml/2floz olive oil
- 100g/4oz grated Cheddar cheese
- 50g/2oz freshly grated Parmesan cheese
- chopped fresh parsley, to garnish

Bring a large saucepan of water to the boil and add the fusilli with a dash of olive oil. Cook for about 10 minutes, stirring occasionally, until tender. Drain, return to the saucepan and set aside.

Preheat the oven to 200°C/400°F/Gas Mark 6. Arrange the chunks of pepper on a baking sheet and place under a hot grill for about 5 minutes, or until slightly charred.

Mix the pepper into the pasta with the remaining ingredients and toss together to combine. Transfer to an ovenproof dish and bake for about 15 minutes, or until heated through and the cheese has melted. Sprinkle over the chopped parsley and serve.

Cheesy Pepper Supper

Based on a traditional macaroni cheese, this colourful, tasty supper is a great dish for kids.

SERVES 4–6

- 225g/8oz dried macaroni
- ½ red pepper, seeded and finely diced
- ½ yellow pepper, seeded and finely diced
- dash of olive oil

FOR THE SAUCE:

- 50g/2oz butter
- 50g/2oz plain flour
- 575ml/1pt milk
- 10ml/2tsp French mustard
- 25g/1oz grated Cheddar cheese
- salt and freshly ground black pepper

FOR THE TOPPING:

- 100g/4oz fresh breadcrumbs
- 50g/2oz grated Cheddar cheese

Bring a large saucepan of water to the boil and add the macaroni with the diced peppers and a dash of olive oil. Cook for about 10 minutes, stirring occasionally, until tender. Drain and transfer to a shallow ovenproof dish. Set aside. Preheat the oven to 200°C/400°F/Gas Mark 6.

To make the sauce, melt the butter in a large saucepan and stir in the flour to make a paste. Gradually stir in the milk, a little at a time, until evenly blended, with no lumps.

Gently bring the sauce to the boil, stirring constantly, until thickened. Stir in the mustard and cheese and season with salt and pepper. Continue to cook for a further 1–2 minutes, until the cheese has melted.

Pour the cheese sauce over the macaroni and pepper mixture and mix it in with a spoon. When the sauce and pasta are evenly combined, sprinkle over the topping ingredients and bake for 25–30 minutes, until crisp and golden.

Gnocchetti Sardi with Broccoli and Tomatoes

A lovely light lunch or supper dish. Choose vivid green, tightly packed heads of broccoli and cook as briefly as possible to retain the colour and crisp texture.

SERVES 4

- 350g/12oz dried gnocchetti sardi (small dumpling shapes)
- dash of olive oil
- 75g/3oz unsalted butter
- 350g/12oz small broccoli florets
- 1 clove of garlic, chopped
- 2tsp chopped fresh rosemary
- 2tsp chopped fresh oregano
- salt and freshly ground black pepper
- 200g/7oz can chopped tomatoes
- 15ml/1tbsp tomato purée
- fresh herbs, to garnish

Bring a large saucepan of water to the boil and add the gnocchetti sardi with a dash of olive oil. Cook for about 6 minutes, stirring occasionally, until tender. Drain and return to the saucepan, covered, to keep warm.

Meanwhile, melt the butter in a large frying pan. Add the broccoli, garlic, rosemary and oregano and season with salt and freshly ground black pepper. Cover and cook gently for about 5 minutes, until tender.

Add the chopped tomatoes and tomato purée and stir. Add the gnocchetti sardi, mix together lightly, then serve immediately, garnished with fresh herbs.

Buckwheat Noodles with Savoy Cabbage

Buckwheat noodles, known as "pizzoccheri", are a speciality of northern Italy, they are available from specialist delicatessens. Wholewheat or egg tagliatelle make good substitutes.

SERVES 6

- 350g/12oz dried buckwheat noodles
- 225g/8oz savoy cabbage, shredded
- 225g/8oz potatoes, peeled and diced
- dash of olive oil
- 150g/5oz unsalted butter
- 2 cloves of garlic, chopped
- 4tbsp chopped fresh sage
- pinch of freshly grated nutmeg
- 200g/7oz diced Fontina cheese
- 100g/4oz freshly grated Parmesan cheese

Bring a large saucepan of water to the boil and add the buckwheat noodles, cabbage and potatoes with a dash of olive oil. Cook for 10–15 minutes, stirring occasionally, until tender. Drain and set aside, covered, to keep warm.

Meanwhile, melt the butter in a large frying pan and sauté the garlic and sage for about 1 minute. Remove from the heat and set aside.

Place a layer of the pasta and vegetables in a warm serving dish and sprinkle with a little nutmeg, some of the Fontina cheese and some of the Parmesan cheese.

Repeat the layers, then pour over the hot garlic butter. Mix lightly into the pasta and serve immediately.

Gnocchetti Sardi with Broccoli and Tomatoes.

Pasta-stuffed Cabbage Leaves

Easy to prepare and sure to impress the guests, this dish can be made the day before and kept in the refrigerator. Allow an extra 15–20 minutes to reheat in the oven before serving.

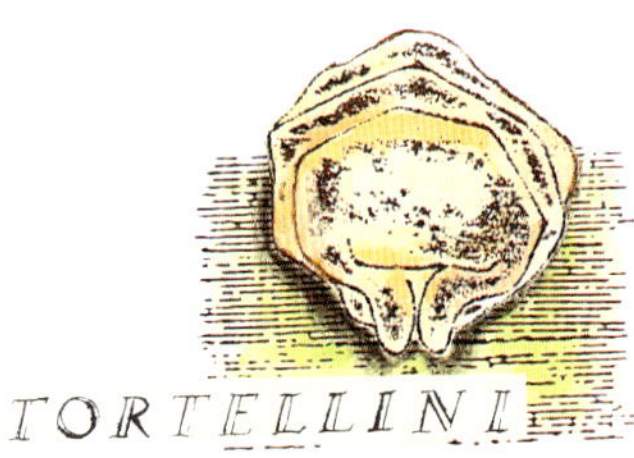

SERVES 4

75g/3oz dried gnocchetti sardi (dumpling shapes) and/or pastina (any tiny shapes)

dash of olive oil

8 large savoy cabbage leaves, stalks removed

FOR THE FILLING:

30ml/2tbsp olive oil

2 cloves of garlic, crushed

2 carrots, peeled and grated

2 courgettes, grated

4 tomatoes, skinned, deseeded and chopped

50g/2oz chopped walnuts

salt and freshly ground black pepper

FOR THE SAUCE:

400g/14oz can chopped tomatoes

60ml/4tbsp dry red wine

150ml/¼pt vegetable stock

1tbsp dried oregano

1 onion, very finely chopped

salt and freshly ground black pepper

Bring a large saucepan of water to the boil and add the pasta with a dash of olive oil. Cook for about 10 minutes, stirring occasionally, until tender. Drain and set aside.

Blanch the cabbage leaves in boiling water, then quickly immerse in cold water and drain. Pat dry with absorbent kitchen paper and set aside.

To make the filling, heat the olive oil in a large frying pan and sauté the garlic for about 1 minute. Add the grated carrots and courgettes and cook for a further 3–4 minutes, stirring occasionally, until tender.

Add the chopped tomatoes, walnuts and pasta. Season with salt and freshly ground black pepper. Cook for about 5 minutes, stirring occasionally, then set aside to cool.

To make the sauce, place all the ingredients in a saucepan and bring to simmering point. Cook for 20–30 minutes, stirring occasionally, until reduced and thickened. Allow to cool slightly, then transfer to a food processor or blender and purée until smooth. Set aside. Preheat the oven to 200°C/400°F/Gas Mark 6.

To assemble the stuffed cabbage leaves, lay the blanched leaves out on the work surface, concave side uppermost, and divide the mixture between the leaves, placing it in the centre of each. Fold the edges of each leaf over to completely encase the filling, securing with a cocktail stick.

Arrange the stuffed leaves in a shallow ovenproof dish and pour the sauce around the edges. Cover with aluminium foil and bake for about 20 minutes, until heated through. Serve immediately, with any extra sauce served separately.

Cannelloni with Greens and Walnuts

Serve with a simple crisp, fresh salad to complement the rich, cheesy sauce and walnut filling. Fresh spinach is a good alternative for this recipe.

SERVES 4

12 dried cannelloni (tubes)

dash of olive oil

butter, for greasing

50g/2oz walnuts, chopped

FOR THE FILLING:

45ml/3tbsp olive oil

1 large onion, chopped

1 clove of garlic, crushed

450g/1lb spring greens, shredded

200g/7oz can chopped tomatoes

1tsp dried oregano

3tbsp chopped fresh basil

225g/8oz ricotta cheese

75g/3oz fresh wholemeal breadcrumbs

50g/2oz walnuts

good pinch of freshly grated nutmeg

salt and freshly ground black pepper

FOR THE CHEESE SAUCE:

25g/1oz butter

25g/1oz plain flour

275ml/½pt milk

50g/2oz grated Fontina cheese

Bring a large saucepan of water to the boil and add the cannelloni with a dash of olive oil. Cook for about 10 minutes, stirring occasionally, until tender. Drain and rinse under cold running water. Drain again, then pat dry with absorbent kitchen paper and set aside.

To make the filling, heat the olive oil in a large frying pan and sauté the onion and garlic for 2–3 minutes, until the onion has softened. Add the spring greens, tomatoes and oregano. Continue to cook for about 5 minutes, stirring frequently, until the liquid has completely evaporated. Remove from the heat and leave to cool.

Place the spring greens mixture in a food processor or blender and add the basil, ricotta cheese, breadcrumbs, walnuts and nutmeg. Purée until smooth, then season with salt and freshly ground black pepper.

To make the sauce, melt the butter in a saucepan. Stir in the flour and cook for 1 minute. Gradually stir in the milk, and heat until bubbling and thickened. Stir in the grated Fontina cheese.

Preheat the oven to 190°C/375°F/Gas Mark 5. Butter the insides of a shallow ovenproof dish. Using a teaspoon, stuff each cannelloni with the filling then lay it in the dish.

Pour the cheese sauce evenly over the cannelloni. Sprinkle with walnuts and bake for about 30 minutes, until bubbling and golden.

TIP:

Sheets of fresh lasagne can be used instead of dried cannelloni. Make up ½ quantity Pasta Dough (page 8) and roll out to 5mm/¼inch thick. Cut into 10 × 15cm/4 × 6inch rectangles and spoon some of the filling along the short end of the sheet of pasta. Roll it up into a neat tube and place in the dish with the sealed end underneath.

Pasta Paella

Based on the classic recipe, this dish makes a delicious, nutritious alternative, using pasta as the main ingredient. Any pasta shape will do; even add a combination of shapes for extra texture.

SERVES 6–8

- 450g/1lb dried farfalle (bows)
- 1tsp ground turmeric
- dash of olive oil, plus 45ml/3tbsp
- 2 cloves of garlic, crushed
- 1 Spanish onion
- 1 red pepper, seeded and chopped
- 100g/4oz baby carrots
- 100g/4oz baby sweetcorn
- 100g/4oz mangetout
- 100g/4oz fresh asparagus tips
- 75g/3oz black olives
- 15g/½oz plain flour

Bring a large saucepan of water to the boil and add the farfalle with the ground turmeric and a dash of olive oil. Cook for about 10 minutes, stirring occasionally, until tender. Drain, reserving the cooking liquid, and set aside.

Heat the remaining olive oil in a large frying pan and sauté the garlic and onion for about 3 minutes, until softened. Add the red pepper, carrots and sweetcorn and stir to combine. Cook for 2–3 minutes, then stir in the mangetout, asparagus tips, black olives and farfalle. Cook for 2–3 minutes, then sprinkle the flour over and mix into the vegetable mixture. Cook for 1 minute, then gradually stir in 425ml/¾pt of the reserved pasta cooking liquid. Cook for 2–3 minutes, until the sauce is bubbling and thickened. Serve straight from the pan or transfer to a warmed serving dish.

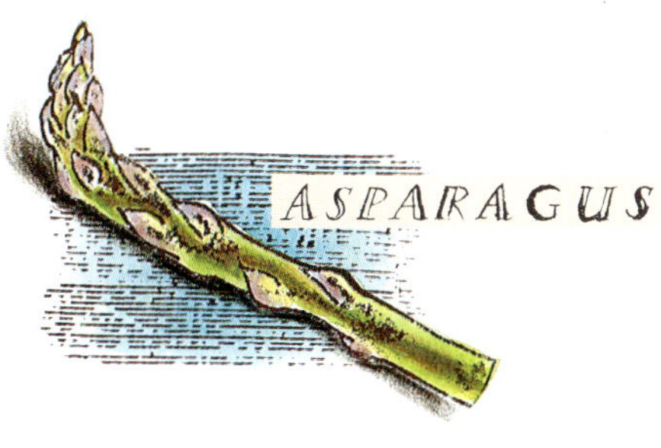

Tagliarini with Green Beans and Garlic

A delicious summer salad, hot main course or vegetable accompaniment, this dish is suitable for almost any occasion.

SERVES 4–6

- 350g/12oz dried tagliarini (flat spaghetti)
- dash of olive oil, plus 60ml/4tbsp
- 350g/12oz haricot beans, topped and tailed
- 225g/8oz potato, cut into 1cm/½inch cubes
- 3 cloves of garlic, chopped
- 5tbsp chopped fresh sage
- salt and freshly ground black pepper
- freshly grated Parmesan cheese, to serve

Bring a large saucepan of water to the boil and add the tagliarini with a dash of olive oil. Cook for about 10 minutes, stirring occasionally, until tender. Drain and set aside.

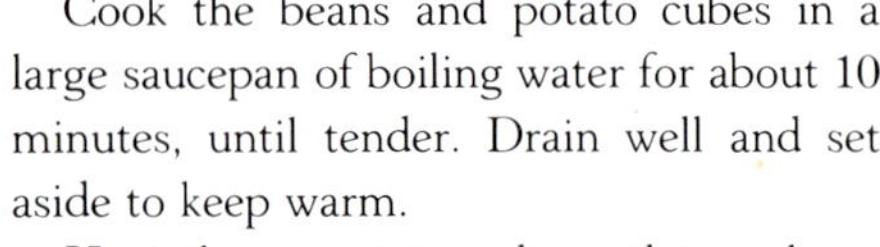
Cook the beans and potato cubes in a large saucepan of boiling water for about 10 minutes, until tender. Drain well and set aside to keep warm.

Heat the remaining olive oil in a large frying pan, add the garlic and sage and season with salt and freshly ground black pepper. Sauté for 2–3 minutes, then add the cooked beans and potato. Cook for 1–2 minutes, then add the cooked tagliarini and mix well.

Cook for about 5 minutes, stirring occasionally, then transfer to a warmed serving dish. Sprinkle with freshly grated Parmesan cheese and serve.

Fettuccine with Garlicky Creamed Spinach

This tasty recipe is quick and easy to prepare. Serve immediately with plenty of freshly grated Parmesan cheese.

SERVES 4–6

- 450g/1lb dried fettuccine
- dash of olive oil
- 25g/1oz butter
- 3 cloves of garlic, crushed
- 450g/1lb frozen chopped spinach, thawed and well drained
- 275ml/½pt single cream
- pinch of freshly grated nutmeg
- salt and freshly ground black pepper
- 50g/2oz freshly grated Parmesan cheese, plus extra to serve

Bring a large saucepan of water to the boil and add the fettuccine with a dash of olive oil. Cook for about 8 minutes, stirring occasionally, until tender. Drain and set aside, covered, to keep warm.

Melt the butter in a large frying pan and sauté the garlic for 1–2 minutes, then add the spinach. Cook over medium heat for about 5 minutes, stirring frequently, until the moisture has evaporated.

Add the cream and nutmeg and season with salt and freshly ground black pepper. Toss in the fettuccine and Parmesan cheese, stir and cook for a final minute. Serve with extra freshly grated Parmesan cheese.

Asparagus Ravioli with Tomato Sauce

A dinner-party dish which can be made in advance – the ravioli can even be put in the freezer several weeks before the party and cooked from frozen. The sauce can be made several hours ahead and reheated before serving.

SERVES 6

- ⅔ quantity Pasta Dough with 15ml/1tbsp tomato purée beaten into the eggs
- 1 quantity Tomato Sauce
- 1 egg, beaten, for brushing
- dash of olive oil
- chopped fresh herbs, to garnish

FOR THE FILLING:

- 30ml/2tbsp olive oil
- 1 clove of garlic, crushed
- 1 onion, very finely chopped
- 225g/8oz fresh asparagus, very finely chopped
- salt and freshly ground black pepper

Keep the fresh pasta dough covered with clingfilm at room temperature and the Tomato Sauce in a saucepan, ready to reheat before serving.

To make the filling, heat the olive oil in a frying pan and sauté the garlic and onion for about 3 minutes, until the onion has softened. Add the chopped fresh asparagus and season with salt and freshly ground black pepper. Sauté the asparagus mixture for about 10 minutes, until softened. Set aside and allow to cool completely.

To make the ravioli, cut the pasta dough in half. Roll out one half to a rectangle slightly larger than 35 × 25cm/14 × 10inches. Trim the edges of the dough neatly. Cover the rectangle with the clingfilm to prevent it drying out. Roll out the other half of the dough to the same measurements. Do not trim the edges.

Place half teaspoonfuls of the filling mixture in lines, spaced about 2cm/¾inch apart, all over the trimmed rectangle of pasta dough. Brush the beaten egg lightly, in lines around the filling mixture, to make the square shapes for the ravioli.

Lay the other rectangle of pasta dough on top and, starting at one end, seal in the filling by lightly pressing the dough, pushing out any trapped air and gently flattening the filling, making little packets. Using a sharp knife or pastry wheel, cut down and then across in lines around the filling to make the square ravioli shapes.

To cook the ravioli, bring a large saucepan of water to the boil and add the ravioli with a dash of olive oil. Cook for about 6 minutes, stirring occasionally, until tender. Drain and set aside.

Meanwhile, reheat the Tomato Sauce. Serve the ravioli with the Tomato Sauce, sprinkled with chopped fresh herbs.

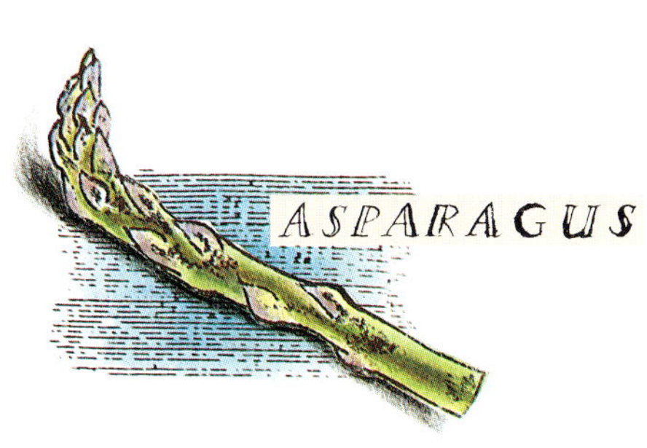

Lentil and Coriander Lasagne

You could make up two or three portions and freeze them uncooked. They cook beautifully from frozen at 190°C/375°F/Gas Mark 5 for 50–60 minutes.

SERVES 1

- 75g/3oz red lentils, washed and drained
- 1 onion, roughly chopped
- 425ml/¾pt boiling water
- 15ml/1tbsp olive oil, plus extra for greasing
- 1 clove of garlic, crushed
- 3tbsp chopped fresh coriander
- 75g/3oz mushrooms, sliced
- 10ml/2tsp sweet soya sauce
- 15ml/1tbsp tomato purée
- salt and freshly ground black pepper
- 1 sheet fresh lasagne (approx 20 × 10cm/ 8 × 4inches), cut in half
- ½ quantity Cheese Sauce
- 25g/1oz grated red Leicester cheese

Place the lentils and chopped onion in a large saucepan and add the boiling water. Bring to the boil, then simmer for about 15 minutes. Drain and set aside. Preheat the oven to 200°C/400°F/Gas Mark 6.

Heat the olive oil in a large frying pan and sauté the garlic and coriander for about 1 minute, then add the sliced mushrooms. Cook for about 4 minutes, then add the sweet soya sauce and tomato purée and season with salt and freshly ground black pepper. Add the cooked lentil mixture, stir and cook gently for about 5 minutes.

To assemble the lasagne, oil a shallow ovenproof dish and place one sheet of the lasagne on the bottom. Cover with half the lentil mixture, then add the other sheet of lasagne. Spoon the remaining lentil mixture over the top, spread out evenly, then pour the Cheese Sauce over the top. Sprinkle with grated cheese then bake for about 20 minutes.

TIP:

This is a perfect opportunity to use up any left-over home-made pasta from another recipe – it is not worth making up a fresh batch for this dish as it uses such a small amount.

Corn and Butter Bean Bake

Canned beans are ideal for this recipe, so take advantage of their convenience.

SERVES 4

- 75g/3oz dried farfallini (tiny bows)
- dash of olive oil
- 45ml/3tbsp sunflower oil
- 2 cloves of garlic, crushed
- 1 onion, very finely chopped
- 3tbsp chopped fresh thyme
- 4 sticks celery, chopped
- 225g/8oz canned butter beans, drained
- 100g/4oz frozen sweetcorn kernels
- 1tbsp plain wholewheat flour
- 275ml/½pt vegetable stock
- salt and freshly ground black pepper

FOR THE TOPPING:

- 2tbsp sesame seeds
- 2tbsp fresh wholewheat breadcrumbs
- sesame oil, to drizzle

Bring a large saucepan of water to the boil and add the farfallini with a dash of olive oil. Cook for about 8 minutes, stirring occasionally, until tender. Drain and set aside. Preheat the oven to 180°C/350°F/Gas Mark 4.

Heat the sunflower oil in a large frying pan and sauté the garlic, onion and fresh thyme for about 3 minutes, until the onion has softened.

Add the chopped celery and cook for about 3 minutes, then add the butter beans and sweetcorn. Cook for about 5 minutes, stirring occasionally, then stir in the flour until evenly blended.

Gradually stir in the vegetable stock, stirring well then season with salt and freshly ground black pepper. Cook for about 5 minutes, then transfer the butter bean mixture to a shallow, ovenproof dish.

In a small bowl, combine the sesame seeds with the breadcrumbs, then sprinkle the mixture over the butter beans. Drizzle over a little sesame oil, then bake for about 20 minutes, until the topping is crisp. Serve immediately.

Sautéed Flageolet Beans with Fusilli

A garlicky dish, made with fresh tarragon to enhance the delicate flavours. Serve as a main course or as an accompaniment.

SERVES 2–4

275g/10oz dried fusilli (short twists)

dash of olive oil, plus 60ml/4tbsp

3 cloves of garlic, crushed

1 large onion, sliced

2tbsp chopped fresh tarragon

400g/14oz can flageolet beans, drained

salt and freshly ground black pepper

Bring a large saucepan of water to the boil and add the fusilli with a dash of olive oil. Cook for about 10 minutes, stirring occasionally, until tender. Drain and set aside.

Heat the olive oil in a large frying pan and sauté the garlic and onion for about 5 minutes, until the onion has browned slightly. Add the tarragon and beans and season with salt and freshly ground black pepper. Cook for 2–3 minutes, then stir in the fusilli. Cook for 3–5 minutes, to heat through. Serve with a crisp green salad.

Winter Stew

You can give this vegetarian dish to carnivores – they'll never notice the lack of meat.

SERVES 4

100g/4oz dried wholewheat radiatori (radiators)

dash of olive oil, plus 30ml/2tbsp

2 cloves of garlic, crushed

1 onion, chopped

450g/1lb carrots, cut into 1cm/½in chunks

225g/8oz button mushrooms

400g/14oz can chopped tomatoes

2 × 400g/14oz cans red and black kidney beans, drained

275ml/½pt vegetable stock

1tbsp paprika

30ml/2tbsp sweet soya sauce

salt and freshly ground black pepper

1tbsp cornflour

Bring a large saucepan of water to the boil and add the radiatori with a dash of olive oil. Cook for about 10 minutes, stirring occasionally, until tender. Drain and set aside.

Heat the remaining olive oil in a large saucepan and sauté the garlic and onion for about 3 minutes, stirring occasionally. Add the carrots and cook for about 5 minutes.

Add the mushrooms and continue to cook for about 3 minutes, stirring occasionally, until slightly softened. Add the remaining ingredients except the cornflour and stir in the radiatori. Cover and cook gently for about 15 minutes, until the vegetables are tender.

In a small bowl, mix the cornflour with a little of the cooking liquid to make a smooth paste. Add the cornflour paste to the stew. Stir and allow to boil again, stirring constantly, until thickened. Cook for a final 3 minutes before serving.

Sautéed Flageolet Beans with Fusilli.

Continental Lentil Soup

Canned lentils make this soup even easier to prepare. They are available from most good delicatessens.

SERVES 4–6

- 50g/2oz butter
- 2 cloves of garlic, crushed
- 75g/3oz dried pastina (any tiny shapes)
- 4tbsp finely chopped fresh parsley
- 400g/14oz can brown lentils, drained
- 1.4l/2½pt vegetable stock
- salt and freshly ground black pepper
- freshly grated Parmesan cheese, to serve (optional)

Melt the butter in a large saucepan and sauté the garlic for about 2 minutes, stirring occasionally.

Add the pastina and chopped parsley and stir. Cook for a further 2–3 minutes, then add the lentils and stock and season with salt and freshly ground black pepper.

Bring the soup to the boil, then reduce the heat and simmer for about 15 minutes. Serve with a little freshly grated Parmesan cheese, if wished.